You Are A Gift

YOU ARE A GIFT

*Twenty Steps to Build Self-Esteem and Move
Toward Realizing Your Dreams*

DARREL HOOVER

To order additional copies of this book, contact:
Xlibris Corporation
1-888-795-4274
www.Xlibris.com
Orders@Xlibris.com
43729

CONTENTS

1. I'm Enough 13

2. I'm Valuable 19

3. I Can Do It 26

4. I'm Moving Forward 30

5. I'm Accomplished 34

6. This Is a New Day 37

7. My Faith Is Rekindled 40

8. I Like Myself 43

9. Why Should I Worry? 46

10. If I Make a Mistake, I Correct It and Move On 48

11. I'll Like You If You Want 50

12. I'm Governed by My Thinking 53

13. I'm Forgiven and You Are Too 55

14. This Is the Best Day of My Life 58

15. I'm on a Mission to Share that You Are Like Me and
    We Are Enough 64

16. Take a Look Outside You 66

17. Your Hope of the Future 70

18. Communication Is the Key to Good Relationships 72

19. When You're Down, Look Up 77

20. Share with Your Best Friend 79

This book is dedicated to . . .

Brent, Debbie, Ashlyn, Camille and Brady Hoover
Angela, Chris, Kaylie and Matthew Abel
and Karen Hoover
Who are all gifts to me.

ACKNOWLEDGEMENTS

THANKS TO DR. William Brown, Metairie, LA, my primary care physician, who is also a gifted photographer. He used his gifts to photograph the butterflies shown on the front and back cover.

Thanks also to all who provided inspiration for this book, especially those who have been quoted and whose stories have been told.

PROLOGUE

DO YOU HAVE a desire to do something out of the ordinary, something special, and something that will contribute to yourself and others?

Does something keep holding you back and preventing you from taking the first step toward the goal of realizing your dreams? This book is meant to inspire you to look at the things in your life that are roadblocks and to move past them. It is also meant to help you start taking "baby" steps toward your goals, even if you are not in a position to "run" toward the finish line!

I was always encouraging my family members to write a book and put all of their thoughts and experiences in print. Then one day, I became inspired by a story I read about the Korean conflict. I began research on this topic and started writing a novel. Although it took me five years to finish the book and get it published, the act of writing a little every weekday morning helped me be more effective in my day job. And I finally reached the finish line when my book *Just One More Day* was published in 2006.

Your goal may not be writing a book, but you may have a dream that you've kept tucked away because you thought there was no chance of making it come true.

My hope is that this book, *You Are a Gift*, will inspire you to take the first step toward realizing the gifts that you possess and start fulfilling your dreams.

CHAPTER 1

I'm Enough

(Everyone, especially teenagers, should read this!)

HOW DO YOU see yourself? Always trying harder, doing more and more, trying to perform better, look better, compete more effectively, become something you would like to be and always wondering if you are enough?

I have good news! You are enough—see yourself as enough. You might think that this is narcissistic or vain.

Stop now and affirm that you are a gift, that you are okay. And that if you accept yourself, there will be others who accept you as you are. You are enough.

1. See the gifts you possess and write as if you are a third party looking on—someone who recognizes your strengths and value. Spend five minutes writing a journal about the gift you bring to life. Filter out any negative thoughts. This may be difficult for you to do, but discipline yourself to write like a person who would give you wise counsel about the value you bring to life. Look at your writing as the beginning of the most adventurous trip you ever planned.

_____

_____

_____

_____

_____

_____

_____

_____

_____

Maybe you don't feel good about the gifts that you wrote about, but in time maybe you will. It can become the first step toward a new journey that can take you where you can make the best contribution. I want to tell you a secret—you are enough the way you are. If you want to make improvements, make changes, and grow in skills and in other ways, that's okay. But remember, do it out of abundance and not out of deficit.

If you set up a standard by using someone else and gauging yourself as less than the standard, you will always evaluate yourself as not enough. You will not celebrate your worth and your value to yourself and others.

Stop again and write down persons that build you up as a person even if they no longer living. Write down their strengths, what you admire about them. Make plans to get with each one that is still living as the opportunity arises so you can build a closer relationship. Also, write about their gifts. This will help you begin to realize your own abilities, gifts, and value. Sometimes we uphold other people's abilities but negate our own.

_____

_____

_____

_____

_____

_____

_____

_____

Now write those negative thoughts you have about yourself that drag you down. Just spend five minutes with this exercise. Decide that you are going to throw this thinking in the trash by writing these on a separate piece of paper then throw it away. When these negatives hit you again, remind yourself that you threw these negatives in the trash—they are not applicable anymore.

_____

_____

_____

_____

_____

DARREL HOOVER

The following is an example of a person who was controlled by his negative thoughts that came from childhood.

Irwin Shaw in his novel *The Top of the Hill* tells the story about the main character, Michael, who at twelve overheard his aunt saying to his grandmother, "She [his mother] is devouring him. We must find her a lover—or at least a husband, or he'll turn out to be the most doleful fat mess we've ever seen. He [Michael] had resolved then and there that one day he would show them all."

As an adult, Michael went skydiving even though his wife begged him not to and questioned what he was trying to prove. Two of his buddies died during the foursome jump, but he told his wife he was going to keep skydiving.

Michael was trying to overcome the smothering he had felt from his overprotective mother who raised him to stay away from risks. He was trying to prove that he was an okay man. The words his aunt had said years before had haunted him, and he thought he had something to prove.

I have a question for you. Are you trying to prove to anyone that you are OK—that you are valuable? Go back to the beginning and review the first few statements that need to saturate your entire heart and mind. This journey you are on may be a long one, but well worth the trip, moving forward in your life toward the life you are passionate about.

Take for example teenagers who put a tremendous stress on themselves and their peer group by trying to be a part of the crowd. When anyone stands out because they are somewhat different from the group, they may face isolation from the group. They live with all their thoughts, dreams, and aspirations handcuffed because they feel that they are isolated from the group.

Isolated people, whether teenager or adult, hope that someone will come along and accept them as they are—letting them know that they are enough. Taken to the extreme, adolescents can contribute to these isolated teens becoming juvenile delinquents—even terrorizing a school to get noticed and respected.

Another example is Albert Einstein. He was not seen as a good fit for school by one of his teachers and later was seen as a total misfit. When Einstein became a physicist, he was looked upon many times with disdain, especially when he introduced the physics theory of relativity. Surveying the findings of other scientists as well as his own findings, he believed in himself and in his theory.

If we think like Einstein thought, we can say, "I'm enough." Once you relax into "I'm enough," you realize that the master designer, who was your architect, brought you into the world as enough. This is an important place to start in your life, giving you confidence to move forward and discover your gifts.

What if when a baby was born, attached to the baby's name was "I will accept you when you are enough?" This is a ridiculous thought; however, we do that to ourselves and others. Judgments are made from what we feel about ourselves. One of the biggest challenges that all of us face is the answer to the question "Am I enough?"

Here's a good exercise. Write your answer to "Am I enough?" Then if you answer that you think you are not enough, write out what it would take for you to be complete. This could be the most important exercise that you could do. Spend ten minutes on this in a private place where you can feel free to put down your honest thoughts. Oh, by the way, don't share your journal even with your best friend for the time being. You do not need anyone's opinion regarding what you are writing in the exercises. If you find that you are extremely down on yourself, by all means, share with someone whom you trust to let them know that you are going through some tough times—that you are distraught. This is a very important part of moving ahead.

_____

_____

_____

_____

_____

_____

_____

_____

DARREL HOOVER

You may want to use a notebook and keep it in a private place as you journal.

Sometimes there are conversations where several mothers compare their children's development. One may say, "My junior crawled when he was only six months." Another will chime in with a one-up on the six-month crawler. On and on it goes comparing their children's development. Some mother may go away from the group feeling that her child is way behind and wondering what is wrong with the child—all the time forgetting that each child develops at his or her own pace.

It is at this point that the mother must be thankful for the progress that her child is making and not worry about the other children who may be slower or faster in developing. Remember that your child begins to pick up how you feel about him or her. It is a good time to establish that your child is enough!

Remember, if you can draw back the curtains and see your gifts that will bring rewards, happiness, and contentedness, you will be more apt to share in the joy of others.

Following this question leads to asking "Are you enough?" Hundreds of years ago, a great theologian named Thomas Aquinas said, "Man will never rest until he rests in Thee." I want to add another thought by modifying this. You will never accept yourself as enough until you rest with the thought "I'm enough."

How do you go about engaging this thought and making it a part of your daily life? Well, the next chapter will help you explore this.

Listed below are opportunities for you to explore the times when you thought you were enough.

1. Write down an experience or experiences that occurred where you felt good about what you did or achieved—*you were enough.*

   _____
   _____
   _____
   _____
   _____

2. What did you feel, and how did that affect your day?

_____

_____

_____

_____

_____

3. What if you could remember these experiences when you faced a challenge where you felt overwhelmed and that you were not enough? What difference do you think it would make with you if you pressed on through the tough challenge?

_____

_____

_____

_____

_____

4. Since you have written down these experiences, a good action to reinforce what you wrote is to share this with a close friend.

CHAPTER 2

I'm Valuable

(Adults, be sure to read this chapter. Also, find a young person and share this idea—you may make an impact on the rest of this young life.)

E ACH PERSON IS valuable. Everyone has something to bring to this earth. We are all born to succeed and to bring something to the world that contributes to making this world a better place. Success is relative since each person views success differently.

Tina B. Tessina, PhD, LMFT, put it this way, "Each of us is a special package, a gift to the planet. If you're looking for a reason for your life, look into your gifts. The whole point is to discover what you have to give, and to give it as effectively as possible."

The book *The Marks of an Educated Man* by Albert Wiggam was one of my dad's favorite books. This book made a deep impression on my life. The theme of the book is that no matter what grade you finished in grade school, high school, or college, it is what you do with what you have and your situation that causes you to be an educated man. So express your gift in the situation you find yourself.

Remember Abraham Lincoln's challenges? He taught himself, became a lawyer, failed at several elections for government office, but he was elected president later in his life. By our standards today, with such emphasis on getting formal education, his resume would not have gotten him very far. However, he certainly was an educated man.

He expressed the gift of standing up for the truth wherever it took him—eventually leading the United States through one of the most brutal wars ever. During the Civil War his goal was to bring the nation back together.

The way you were treated while growing up has a tremendous effect on whether you believe you are valuable. We have roots in the attitudes of those who first nurtured us into this world. Psychologists suggest that the first six years of our lives are the most formative years of development—our personalities are formed, and our beliefs about ourselves are formed. New thought says that in infancy up to age three, the personality is formed.

Even today, some experts say, "At birth the personality is in place." Of course a good nurturing environment brings out the gifts that are already there.

The years that follow reflect what you were exposed to, until you have a crisis that causes you to take a closer look at yourself. If you discover how unique you are, then you are able to feel valuable. If you stay with beliefs that are negative about yourself, a lifetime of living will not overcome these beliefs.

I've aforementioned Einstein, the great physics mind. He was told that he would not succeed in school because he was a poor student. What caused him to become one of the most brilliant minds of our time? Somewhere along the way, someone discovered his gift and encouraged him to proceed to share his gift. What if he had believed the teacher who said that he was not going to accomplish much in life? We would have lost the benefits of one of the greatest gifted persons of the world.

Another example of a successful scientist is George Washington Carver, who discovered the multiple uses of the peanut and revolutionized the world of agriculture. Although he was born at a time when it was hard for him to get an education, he rallied and became an outstanding scientist. Why? Someone affirmed his gift and challenged him to realize his potential. Thus, his contribution to the world was not only that of a great scientist, but a role model as a person who didn't let obstacles get in the way of expressing his gift.

You have heard persons state what they will do if they win the lottery. You do not have to win a lot of money to start the journey of realizing your dreams. Whatever your circumstance, start by doing what you are meant to do, but don't delay. No matter what circumstance, start today by taking steps toward realizing your dream. Even small steps toward your passions will begin an exciting journey.

DARREL HOOVER

Why not stop reading for a moment and think about some of the obstacles you face? You may be clouding your opportunities by letting obstacles keep you from expressing your gifts. Write what you think may be some obstacles you have.

_____

_____

_____

_____

_____

Write some of your thoughts in your journal. Remember, a journal is about your thoughts, dreams, fears, and experiences, but remember a journal is not a diary.

My grandson had a great challenge at an early age in learning to walk. He learned to walk with a walker that his dad nicknamed a "scooter." My grandson would take off on the sidewalk with his "scooter" and get way ahead of his family as if he were winning in the walk toward the destination.

Since he called his walker a "scooter," his friends started wanting a scooter. Because his dad and mom had given him much encouragement to learn to walk, he soon learned to walk without the scooter.

Oddly enough, he would run many times wherever he was going. What a way to celebrate something that was a great challenge!

When he was six or so, he visited our home when we were living outside Washington DC. He had long since learned to walk without the scooter. While on the metro train traveling to DC, he stood in the aisle and said, "I'm winning," because he was able to balance himself without holding on as the metro rocked back and forth and started and stopped. Persons around him smiled and were inspired to see a boy who was able to accomplish the smallest feat say, "I'm winning."

We all have challenges to overcome to be able to express the gift that has been given to us. What is your dream, your passion that you would like to move toward? You might not be able to exit your day job, but you can start working each day toward your passion—in due time you might be able to go full time following your dream.

_____

_____

_____

_____

_____

As an example, I recently met a man who gave up his real estate broker business in Texas to move to New Orleans. He enrolled in a seminary to learn better how to be a prison chaplain. Although he wanted to continue to do full-time real estate, he wanted to work as a chaplain part time. He was skilled in real estate, but he was passionate about ministering to inmates. What a great example of a person moving toward his passion without jeopardizing his income.

I mentioned in the prologue about the book I wrote. While writing that book, many times I wondered what I was doing writing a novel when I had never even written an article for a newspaper. I thought that authoring was something other people did and undervalued the passion I had for the story I was writing. I learned that if no one but me enjoyed the book, it was enough.

To the contrary, I learned that there were persons who enjoyed reading it. Some were inspired. Some were moved to tears. Others saw it as a spiritual journey. Many never responded as to what their thoughts were about the book. But it didn't matter, because the book was enough.

I began to wonder what I could do to encourage others to write about their thoughts, their stories, their lives, or to create a novel. I have met many who want to write their stories but don't know how to get started. So I began giving seminars with the title "Discovering the Book Inside of You."

I was leading one of these seminars, when a gentlemen said that he had a completed book but needed to get it published. Its theme was that he began traveling the globe to find himself—his gifts. After a few weeks, I received an e-mail from him that he had it published as a result of the seminar. He was so excited that his dream was realized. Although he was in the engineering field, he became reignited in finding that he had realized a dream by unlocking the door of opportunity.

Recently, a lady who was a new writer brought her friend along to a seminar. "You have a book within you," she told her friend. As the seminar progressed, her friend got excited about writing stories. I shared about writing what you see and have experienced, since nobody has experienced what you have experienced—your experiences are unique to you. A lightbulb turned on in her. She left ready to begin expressing her stories on paper.

You will have stories that will inspire others, encourage them, and add value to their lives. Remember, you are valuable, and your experiences are only yours. We need to hear about your life experiences that will add meaning to our lives.

Writing the book *Just One More Day*, became a joyful daily hobby. I would go to the coffee shop and write every morning before going to work. After I had written for about thirty to forty-five minutes, I was motivated to go to my day job. The joy of writing carried over to every part of my life.

Each time I write, this excitement reignites, and I look forward to the time I can express myself in print.

I read an article where three photographers traveled to New Orleans to take pictures of the Hurricane Katrina devastation. While there, they established a group to help New Orleans youth to go out and photograph some of the scenes that attracted them. It became therapy for these young students.

Sensing the mission of reconstructing New Orleans, they relocated to New Orleans and began helping youth cope by expressing themselves through photography, adding their own thoughts in response to their work in New Orleans. They are now expressing a new passion for helping those who have been through tragedy. Through helping people in the disaster, they discovered some of their own gifts.

Celebrating the gift of others may uncover some of our gifts. All around us are opportunities to help ignite the gifts that people have and help them celebrate their uniqueness. When we remember the challenges that we have faced and persons who helped us be overcomers, we become more aware of the opportunities to help those around us.

The following questions should help you understand the challenges you might have faced in growing up.

As a young child, what are some of the things an adult said to you that made a lasting impression?

_____
_____
_____
_____
_____

Are the memories good?

_____
_____
_____
_____
_____

Or are they crippling you from being who you could be?

_____
_____
_____
_____
_____

What if you could get past some of these demeaning conversations or experiences you had as a child and move past them to feel valuable?

What if the remembrances are helpful in fulfilling your destiny? Have you moved forward to check out the good feedback?

Do you recall any of these conversations that might help you stay on track in fulfilling your dreams?

CHAPTER 3

I Can Do It

S O OFTEN, JUST before success, many get out of the race. They grow tired of waiting, of running, of persistently moving forward to be knocked back many times. Have you ever heard someone say, "If I had only stuck it out a little longer?"

Recently, I was eating lunch on a park bench, and a young man came up and sat down on the next bench. He was dressed for construction work, had a toolbox with him, and looked like he was ready to be hired. I continued eating and then broke the silence by asking how his work was going. He told me that while he was in Florida, work was hard to find. He was a finish carpenter, a welder, and did a lot of related builder jobs. He seemed to value his skills.

He said every day at a lumber yard he had waited for someone to employ him. That particular day he was asked to leave the lumber yard's parking lot, so he lost his chance of finding work. I asked if he had eaten. He replied that he hadn't, so I gave him a few dollars. Also, I asked him to call me the next day. I said I would ask around to see if I could help him get employment.

When I arrived at work the next day, a note was in my office that said, "Thanks for your help. I have a job." Although he felt temporarily down about what had happened the day before, just a little encouragement helped him reaffirm his value.

What is your first memory of someone encouraging you to do what you could if you had the courage and help? I remember the story my mom read me about the train that said "I think I can" all the way up the hill. Although the hill got tougher for the little train, the train believed that he could move toward the top of the hill—the goal—and he did. I sometimes think of this train when I'm confronted with a challenge.

Yes, there are times when changing directions on a path that is leading to nowhere is wise. However, so often when the going gets tough, we quit or give up. You have seen this in sports. A team plays heroically throughout the game but gives up in the last few minutes and loses.

So what would it take for you to press on? In my profession as a recruiter, I facilitate career seminars. After much planning and work, sometimes there are very few attendees. It would be easy to let these results discourage me from conducting the seminars.

Over time, the career seminars have helped our company recruit many new qualified agents. If I had based my judgment on some of the poor responses from the seminars, I would have lost many opportunities to recruit some qualified candidates. So remember, at first you may have obstacles and want to give up, but you may be close to a turnaround.

The "I-can-do-it" attitude keeps us on track to pursue goals that we deem valuable. It is the pulse of one who is determined to succeed with a worthy goal. If roadblocks come, this attitude will find other paths to pursue goals and realize dreams.

We all remember the story of Thomas Edison, the inventor of the lightbulb. How many times did he fail before he discovered how to get the filament in the lightbulb to continue to give light? A hundred, two hundred tries, or 1,000 tries? No, it was over 1,100 attempts before he reached his goal.

What if Edison had given up after five tries saying, "Been there and done that!" Have you experienced someone who said "been there, done that," and it didn't work? Only one try is their basis that something will not work.

I just talked to a candidate for a career in real estate. She had to take the tests for her license four times. She said, "I didn't stop until I got it done." Although she has been a server in a restaurant for thirty-five years, her objective is to be an outstanding real estate agent. Her friends want her to help them with their real estate needs when she joins a firm.

She must continue to work at her restaurant job until she can get an income in real estate. She has two real estate agents that she can partner with until her real estate business can support her. She said, "I've been waiting tables for thirty-five years, and I know how to treat people." She is in her fifties and still has the I-can-do-it attitude. And I know she will do well because she has the attitude of one who accomplishes her dreams even if they take several decades to complete. Wow, what determination! I wish that all of us would remember that to accomplish anything there is a price you have to pay—persistence and determination toward a worthy goal.

You must look into the future with this question, "What if I continue to work toward my dream?" It certainly will take delayed gratification and persistence to consistently move forward. Can you see your dream and realize that if you plan, implement, and devise action plans to move forward, it is very likely that you will realize your dream? Write what your future looks like when you have achieved your dreams.

_____

_____

_____

_____

_____

_____

_____

One of the benefits of moving toward a dream is that the journey itself becomes a joy. Every morning when I was writing, I felt like I was creating part of a movie. The writing helped me enjoy my workday more because I knew I was achieving my true dream.

I remember many years ago when my wife and I and her parents drove up Pike's Peak. Along the way, the views were awesome. When we saw the snowcapped mountains in the distance, with Christmas trees everywhere, it took our breaths away. As we neared the top of Pike's Peak, our excitement grew. Then, it began to snow, and the snow clouds hung very low. Arriving at the top, the clouds obscured any view.

So the journey is the real deal. That was a lifelong lesson I learned that day. Every moment, every hour, and every day is where life is. It is in the enjoyment of the ride in life that fills our days and makes for an exciting life. Waiting until we arrive at our goal or dream may be uplifting, but the journey toward our goals can be breathtaking.

Therefore, remember that you can realize your dream if that dream is filled with "I can do it." The journey toward the goal may not be the final destination, but the ride toward it will be awesome.

CHAPTER 4

I'm Moving Forward

IN THE *AARP Bulletin* for May/June 2009 is an article, "How Dolly Does It." "'Through it all,' she says, 'there wasn't ever a time I thought I wasn't going to make it.'" This is referring to Dolly Parton.

During her teenage years Parton and her mother's brother, Bill Owens, also a songwriter, would venture into Nashville and try to get signed. "We used to come down in his rickety car any time we could beg, borrow, or steal enough money for gas," Parton remembers. "We'd clean up in service stations. I'd wash my hair in those old, cold sinks and put my makeup on in the mirrors in the car."

Along with hope and faith, Parton always knew the value of keeping the company of folks she trusted. "You're not going to see your dreams come true if you don't put wings, legs, and arms, hands and feet, on 'em," she says. "You gotta have people to help carry out those dreams, and, Lord, I've been surrounded by great people." "That's partly because Parton knows how to avoid negative people," says Ted Miller, her business manager at the Dollywood Company.

Are you ready to put wings, legs, and arms, hands and feet to your dreams? The following story is an example of putting wings and determination to your dreams.

On a scheduled flight to London from Chicago, as we boarded the plane, the flight attendant said that it would be a while before the plane would be able to take off. Have you ever boarded a plane only to find out that there was a problem with the plane's mechanical functions?

I was in charge of a group of youth aboard a 747 jet heading for England from Chicago. The flight attendant came on the loud speaker and said that they had to fly in a part from Denver, Colorado. The plane sat on the tarmac for hours and served as a dining hall and theater. Although we didn't get to take off at the departure time, our nerves were overcome by our excitement of the adventure. There was no reluctance on anyone's part to fly. We were determined to arrive at Heathrow airport in England.

While we were waiting, we ate several meals, watched movies, and enjoyed each other with anticipation of our future destination. You see, the airline realized that we had our sights on moving forward and achieving our goals. They helped us through the challenge of waiting many hours by entertaining us while we waited. Guess what? We knew they would fix the problem, and we would move forward to our destination. We arrived at Heathrow in London and achieved our goal of mission work in England.

Having patience and focusing on your goal are important to moving forward.

So how about starting now to move forward to use your gifts? Every new beginning has a starting point. And every starting point has a point in time to start. And every point in time to start something new must have a motivation. Otherwise, we're stuck in a rut!

So you do not want to stay in a rut. Someone said, "A rut is a grave with ends extended." So everyone, let's take a look at ourselves and inventory if we are moving forward.

What are things that are a rut to you? Certainly, there are repetitive chores that each of us is responsible for; however, each of us can spice up our lives by adding some of the things that we are very interested in and passionate about.

Stop and list the things about you that are a rut in your life.

_____

_____

_____

_____

_____

Although we traditionally think of the New Year as the time to inventory where we have been, where we are going, and planning how to get there, every day can be a new beginning for us to inventory using the same process. It only takes a few minutes to look into the future and visualize what we could do to move forward in our lives.

Ruts tend to help us excuse ourselves from moving forward. All of us can come up with a list of reasons why we don't have time to get out of the rut and add some interesting things to our lives. For example, I enjoy writing. Although this is not my day job, I found that taking a few moments out of the day to write makes the day go much better.

This is a good principle for us all to remember. Find a few minutes each day to spice up your life with some things you would really like to do.

Recently, while conducting the seminar on "Discovering the Book Within You," nine people attended. Out of those nine, one had already completed a book and had it edited. A few weeks later I received an e-mail from the person saying that the book was now getting published. The writer only needed help in being published. Another knew what she wanted to write but needed some help in getting started.

The next day I asked her how it was going with her writing. She said she started on the book after the seminar. She said she didn't spend much time, but she realized that the way to reach her goal was to start writing. What if one of your goals is to travel and learn about other areas?

My wife and I want to tour Alaska, but time and resources prevent that at this time. So I've thought about seeing a movie on Alaska or going to the library and looking through a book of photographs of this enchanting place. We could enlarge our horizons without going there; and per chance we just might find a way at some point to travel to Alaska. Also, we would then have a much better idea of what we want to see and do while we are there.

Again, the time spent investigating the places you want to visit can take you away from the humdrum of everyday responsibilities. Remember, many times the planning and the learning before you go on a trip can be as exciting as the trip. Is it time for you to move forward on some of your interests?

Most of us have heard the question, "What would we do if we could do anything you wanted to do in life without regard to money?" Stop and make a list. Just maybe you could start toward realizing some of your dreams on the list. Remember, the journey of a thousand miles begins with the first step. Put this in your journal notebook. Again, keep these thoughts only to yourself for now. Later, you may want to share these with a trusted friend.

CHAPTER 5

I'm Accomplished

NO MATTER WHAT you do, you are accomplished in something. If you compare yourself to your idol or someone else, you will forever be paralyzed in not believing you are accomplished.

To take a real look at your accomplishments, spend time celebrating the small progress as well as the more rapid progress toward achieving your goals.

After working in my job for eight years, I was recognized by a national recruiting company for outstanding work. However, I didn't see it. There it was, right in front of me. Someone recognized that I'm accomplished, but I had not seen it.

Do we tend to look at the things that we do not accomplish, negating the things we have accomplished? How do we overcome the tendency to see ourselves as not accomplished?

First, let me suggest you look at the achievements in your life or in your work whatever they are. I once had a job where a mentally challenged person was helping me do gofer work. This person brought such excitement to the everyday minutiae that it was catching. His enthusiasm was one of his accomplishments as well as his commitment to doing whatever he could with his limitations. He was an inspiration to all in the office where I worked. His greeting was contagious as he persistently asked, "What's happening?"

When you positively look at where you have been in your life and work, you can get a better perspective of what you have accomplished. I learned this when driving up Pike's Peak and stopping to look over the valley and distant mountain peaks. We could see the twists and turns and the uphill climbs. It was easy to see the progress we had made even though we were only partially up the mountain with a long way to go to reach the peak.

With this in mind, try the following exercise with your lifework. Discipline yourself to look for the progress and the distance covered that got you where you are. Remember that when climbing actual mountain peaks or when working, you must go through twists and turns as you ascend the mountain. Thus it is with your life.

Why is this important to look back at your progress? In watching the Forty-first Super Bowl game in Miami, the pregame show brought out the record of one of the teams. The team had reached the play-offs with a lot of ups and downs. Opinions flared regarding the ability of this team to reach the Super Bowl.

In looking back at their play-off season to get them to the bowl, they realized that their recent accomplishments gave them the foundation to go into the Super Bowl game and win. Had they not looked at their recent accomplishments, they might not have carried their winning attitude into the Super Bowl game in Miami. And by the way, they won.

Recently the Saints from the "Who Dat" nation won Super Bowl after forty-three years. Drew Brees said that when he came to New Orleans in 2006 as quarterback of the Saints, he saw T-shirts that stated, "Faith." He said that he shared with the team that for each letter of faith, it had meaning. F is for fortitude; A is for attitude; I is for integrity; T is for trust; H is for humility. As the team built a foundation on these principles, they would indeed become a united team.

In 2006, I talked with the vice president of a company who asked how my book sales were going. I said a few are selling, but I just haven't had the time to promote it. He said that he was going to contact a national professional magazine and tell them that a top recruiter had written a book.

The writer of the magazine contacted me, and my story ran in March 2007. I had no idea the perception of accomplishment that this vice president saw in my writing a successful book. All I saw was that I didn't have time to promote it due to my responsibilities in my job.

Try to look at your accomplishments from a distance. Step back and detach yourself and look at where you've been, what you've accomplished and celebrate those accomplishments. And like the NFL team who looked back at their accomplishments, it will motivate you to start winning more and more at what you are doing.

There is nothing wrong with celebrating your accomplishments. At the Miami Dolphins game in Miami in 2009, the Saints quarterback Drew Brees ran to the goal post and dunked the football over it after he had just rushed across the goal line. He celebrated! The game had been very intense, and it was unlike Drew to run the football.

However, he wanted the touchdown bad enough to risk running the ball against one of the toughest defenses in pro football. Likewise, you can celebrate the little and big accomplishments in your life. Also learn from your mistakes, but move forward. This is what life is all about. And guess what? You will start looking at others and their accomplishments and celebrating with them. Looking inward like this helps clear your lens to see what others are doing.

Many of us have struggled with this by comparing ourselves with others who have excelled instead of looking at what will propel us forward. Realize that if you travel up a mountain and stop to look at where you have been, you will see new scenery. Let life become a discovery process.

CHAPTER 6

This Is a New Day

YOU MAY HAVE heard the saying, "Today is the first day of the rest of your life." I've often been glib with that statement, never stopping to think through what it might mean. So what might this mean to you?

As you drive along life's highway, if you are looking in the rearview mirror too much, you might cause a wreck by not focusing on what's happening in front of you. It's very similar to carrying around negative baggage from previous experiences.

I have a visual scene of a street person pushing a buggy with all their belongings, which we most likely would classify as trash. I then relate this to the way we carry the past, pushing it into the future, and collecting more bundles of stuff that weigh us down. Not focusing on looking back can help us regain our focus on a real future as well as making today count toward that future.

When I awake each morning, I have started thanking the Lord for sleep during the night and the new morning. A spirit of gratitude helps put a spring in my step as I greet the new day. One morning I began quoting a scripture, and my wife continued it. We went back and forth until the scripture was completed that we both knew. Also, I began singing a chorus, and she continued it, and then I picked up where she left off. It was fun and very uplifting. This was a first with us. I realized that this could be an excellent way to start the day both physically and spiritually.

"Today is the first day of the rest of your life" means that life's bank account gives me a carte blanche to spend the day as I choose. I can spend it wildly with no thought of the destination or where my actions will take me, or I can chart a course that will take me where my dreams point the way. Or I can fill my street basket with yesterdays, trash, and regrets and push along with no thought to a destination.

Rather, the reward of filling my thoughts with plans and actions that move me into the future is exponentially greater as the days pass. The investment has greater returns than a bull market on Wall Street.

Remember when you traded in your old car for a new car with the promise of a better performing vehicle. The aroma of the new car interior was so clean, and it reminded you of a new experience in driving. It probably lifted your spirits as you drove the first few days. What about treating a new day with the same experience?

Suppose you awoke to a new day, a new attitude, a new zeal, and a new purpose for the day. As you go about the day, your day will be brighter, your step lighter, and your life full of purpose. The baggage that was yesterday is left behind. Lessons learned from yesterday are recorded but not carried as regrets and baggage that load you down and keep you from the gift of life today. What a ride that would be!

What do you do to combat bad weather, reversals, disappointments, criticisms, and other challenges that you awake to almost every day? In New Orleans, it is early spring, and it is sunny. This is such a contrast to the cloudy weather that has persisted for almost a month. This weather tends to cloud a person's mind if one lets it. So how do we offset the blues that comes from the challenges?

In a past Super Bowl, during the first play, the Bears ran back a kickoff for a touchdown. After the game the Colts' quarterback was asked how that run had affected the players. He said that they all knew that if they stayed calm and played their game well, they had a great chance to win. Their response dictated the outcome of the game. The Colts won after what initially looked like would be a runaway win by the Bears.

There is a principle in the Colts' attitude: "As a man thinketh, so is he." This comes from the wisdom of the ages found in the book of Proverbs in the Bible. The way one responds to any challenge determines the outcome.

DARREL HOOVER

You have heard the sigh, "Here we go again!" You see, this will predict the failure heard in the sigh. This attitude will guide a person to the blues whether the sun is shining or not. One of the most interesting books I've read regarding negative things that happen is *Failing Forward* by John Maxwell.

It tells the example about how to respond to failure or anything negative that comes your way. The author gives the example of the parents of a baby. What if the parents when they see their baby fall when taking his first steps decide that they'll let the baby crawl since the baby failed to walk without falling? Instead, what do they do? They help the child to try and try again, encouraging the child to take steps toward them when they are only a few feet away. Once the baby makes it a few steps, the parents celebrate the success. Thus it is with any challenge.

You envision success and act as if what you are doing will succeed. See it unfold with the steps it will take to make it happen. Go through the whole process like a fiction writer sees scenes appearing and then put your plans on paper with time lines to realize your vision. What if you fail to achieve your vision? Remember the principle of failing forward. Your failure could be the prelude to your success as you respond by moving forward.

What are the failures you remember that could be stepping stones to successes?

_____
_____
_____
_____
_____
_____
_____
_____

CHAPTER 7

My Faith Is Rekindled

IF I HAD faith as much as grain of mustard seed, I could say to this mountain, "Be moved and it would." While visiting in West Virginia, I saw that some of the mountains jetted straight up like giant boulders. Many cliff climbers would come from all over the globe to test their skills. Then in Virginia there are mountains that are similar to the rolling mountain ranges of the Smokies. They represent an awesome picture of bold beauty. For the scripture to say "If I had faith as a grain of mustard seed, I could say to this mountain, it would be moved" is indeed a power greater than any nuclear bomb that has ever been created.

So often we are so focused at looking within our own circle of work and family that we miss the expanse of the universe and creation happening all around us. One recent night, the sky was all ablaze as the sun poured onto the clouds and lit up the whole horizon with rich shades of red. It was so stunning that I couldn't stop watching. It took me away from the circle of concerns around me and lifted my spirits. I think faith does that producing a power from within that moves us forward—similar to moving mountains.

Faith has a way of hitting its target. Like a guided jet missile, faith hones in on its goal and makes corrections in flight until it reaches its intended goal. Faith is the ongoing energy that is implanted in us to continue in spite of the obstacles that we face until we accomplish our goal. It is always a choice to continue this faith, which reenergizes us as we break through barriers.

Faith attracts others who share the same faith. Others help us as we move forward through whatever impedes our progress. The community of those with faith supports our progress and helps when we are stuck in challenges and can't move forward. The rewards of regaining movement forward toward the goal are incalculable.

Have you ever been going down a trail in the mountains and all you can seek is the canopy of trees? You come into a clearing and see before you miles of mountains on the horizon that are draped with beautiful light blue smoke. You stop, realizing that had you not traversed the tough trail up the mountains surrounded by trees, you would have never been able to see the beautiful sight.

What if you get off the trail and get lost? The mountains take on another view—one of anxiety and worry. How do you get back on the trail and find your way out or how do you get back up from being down?

First, you look back at how you got off the trail. You see how your faith faltered and then seek to find your way back. Then you need to take a deep breath and stop and meditate. Then reactivate your faith. Remember the statement, "If you had faith as much as a grain of mustard seed," and you realize that to activate your faith you need to look up as the Psalmsist says, "I will lift mine eyes unto the hills from which cometh my help." You ask for guidance to see your way back to the trail that leads you forward toward your goal.

Another motivation to activate your faith is to understand the value of the day. Each day is a gift and not to be wasted. The Psalmist in the Old Testament puts it this way, "This is the day the Lord hath made, let us rejoice and be glad in it." When we realize the resources that are available to us to keep us going and alive, we will see the value of our lives in each day.

Many people are struggling with their lives and are off the trail that leads to their goals. They need someone to help them find their way. There is nothing more rewarding than helping another find the way. It has the effect of helping you find your own way.

Although it may be a long way back, realize that you will be back on the trail, the right path, moving toward the goal.

I will never forget the time traveling back from a camp in North Carolina, and it was my shift to drive. We drove out of a gas station, and the passengers went to sleep. As I drove for about an hour, a passenger woke up and looked around discovering that we were going back the way we came. We were only backtracking. So embarrassed, I turned around, and before long we were actually making progress going the correct direction. They never let me forget this.

Sometimes when we are not paying attention, we can go in the wrong direction. Change directions when you get off the path and are going in the wrong direction. Don't fret over getting off the path but quickly make the correction and move forward. It is the lost energy over regrets that can keep you from moving forward.

In the book *The Walk Across America* by Peter and Barbara Jenkins, they relate that after they were married in New Orleans, their goal was to walk to the West Coast. Peter had already walked from New York to New Orleans where he met his bride. They trained well for the walk and then struck out with supplies on their back. After walking for days, they pitched their tent on straw from cut sugarcane. During the night, the drone sounds of mosquitoes kept Peter awake worrying that the cloud of mosquitoes would suck them alive.

After surviving this and many other obstacles, Barbara needed to rest, and Peter was worried about continuing the walk out West. Resolutely, they eventually achieved their goal. This real life story shows how determination can help in accomplishing a meaningful goal. Reading their book will inspire you to forge ahead when there are tough hurdles to cross.

CHAPTER 8

I Like Myself

ACCEPTING YOURSELF UNCONDITIONALLY, with all your faults and strengths, is the foundation to relating to others in a loving way. When you love you, you can love others. Wow, what does that mean? You can go for a lifetime and never share your love unconditionally until you love you.

If you work on yourself to improve, that's great. Certainly, everyone can grow and become a better person. Each one has a personal gift that they can build on and share with others. However, this growth must be based upon a person's self-worth. It is all in your perspective of yourself.

From childhood through adulthood, most suffer from "sitting out" too much of life that has been given to us to enjoy. There is a song that expresses this in a good way. It states that when it's time to dance, don't sit it out—dance. Life is for the living, and to live is to express your gift. It is to get in the game of life and go for it. Only you can decide to get into life and make something of the gift you have been given.

Many times we place restrictions on ourselves and what we will do based upon what others think we ought to do. On a retreat by the ocean, I sailed above the sea doing parasailing. A boat pulled me parallel to the Cancun beach with strong winds that lifted me aloft on a parachute about four hundred feet above the water.

Before launch, a friend tried to ground me by begging me not to do this for fear that it could end in tragedy. I refused to listen. I decided that to get over my fear of heights, I would go up on a parachute being towed by a speedboat. It was an exhilarating experience. It helped free me from such a great fear of heights. Not all the height fears evaporated, but they lessened.

You see, I needed to do this. It helped me deal with issues that were bothering me. What are the areas that you struggle with that you need to take care of? It is very important to take care of yourself by facing those areas in your life that keep you from being your best self.

Recently, in conversation with a young lady, I discovered how difficult it was for her to connect with finding a date. She read many different magazines on how to approach a man in different settings in order to develop a relationship. The lady was attractive with a good personality but with little confidence toward finding a mate. I realized that she did not realize her own uniqueness, much less celebrate her gifts. She did not give off vibes that she cared for herself, but approached the relationship as if she had to become something special for the moment to interest a man in a date.

In contrast to this young lady, a speaker named Dr. Chester Swor spoke at a retreat conference where I was attending. He wobbled to the podium with a cane to steady him; however, he mesmerized the crowd with his enthusiasm and wit. Before the speech was over, every person there seemed to be on the edge of their seats. He had unconditionally accepted himself and loved who he was.

This attitude reverberated throughout the audience. Mixed in with his wit were life illustrations that painted clearly what he was communicating. You came away refreshed and motivated to be your best self simply by his being his best self and sharing the gift given him. Just looking at his physical obstacles, you might think that he would be very dejected about his inability to walk normally. Yet, he loved who he was, accepted himself unconditionally, and the audience responded to his enthusiasm for life.

While I was writing *Just One More Day* and on vacation with my family, I sat by the pool at the motel and met this gentleman who had no legs and was sitting in a wheelchair. Eventually, our conversation turned to the book I was writing. In the book, a GI named Louis reenlisted to go back to Korea to find the South Korean family that saved him. The gentlemen stunned me, telling me that he reenlisted in the Vietnam War to get closer to Korea in order to find his wife. He had a great attitude and was participating in his grandchildren's lives watching them swim and play in the pool. What an inspiration he was. He lost his mobility but not his heart of love for his grandchildren and his life. Although he was unable to find his wife and lost his legs in combat in Vietnam, he found a great love for those around him. His grandchildren were very blessed by his great love for them.

His story amplifies the challenge to accept ourselves, however life may find us, and to press on to continue to give our best self to all around us. So often people mirror back what we give out.

Another example is when my wife and I experienced an unusually gifted waitress who seemed to love her job. We were cutting back our calories, however when dessert time came, she painted the best picture of this alluring desert and smiled from ear to ear. We smiled back and ordered one high-calorie dessert. We responded by mirroring back her excitement over the dessert. She gave her best self to us, and we knew she was the happy person behind the smile—it was written all over her demeanor. She loved who she was and was giving herself away with enthusiasm.

CHAPTER 9

Why Should I Worry?

I N *WEBSTER'S NEW World Dictionary*, it shows that the old English word for worry was wrygan—to strangle. Newer meanings it gives are "to treat roughly, as with continual biting, to pluck at, touch, etc., repeatedly in a nervous way—to worry a loose tooth with the tongue." Another is "to annoy—bother also to cause to feel troubled or uneasy." Others are "a troubled state of mind—anxiety."

Although not in a coma like Dorothy in the *Wizard of Oz*, we are worrying about how to get back to a life that we want. Along the way it is amazing how many different people come along to help point the way back to helping us with the life we want.

My mother grew up in Kansas, in tornado country. Thus after moving to Mississippi, she would take me out when storm clouds came and watch each rolling cloud with diligence. She let me know that she was watching for tornadoes. Storms came and went, but never in my nineteen years at home did one tornado strike. Although it is wise to pay attention to weather, there has always been anxiety in my mind when storm clouds come. I have expended much energy in focusing on calamity during storms.

My wife and I currently live in New Orleans in post-Katrina days. The lady down the street in our quiet neighborhood says she has to leave since she is so afraid of another hurricane coming during the hurricane season. She also stated that although she lives in such a quiet neighborhood, she lives in fear that someone might break in her townhouse. The old English word for *worry* meaning "to strangle" fits her perfectly since her mind is continually nursing her fears like a tongue massaging a bad tooth.

Proverbs states, "As a man thinketh, so is he." Her life is one of perpetual troubled thinking yielding to her fears. She is a worrywart. The dictionary defines a *worrywart* as a person who tends to worry, especially over trivial details.

Yet, we are all susceptible to be overly concerned about so many things. What will the future hold? What about our nation? What about our finances? What about our relationships at home and work? On and on we go. We all face these challenges of deciding if we will yield to the force of worry or keep our focus on faith.

The book of Matthew, in chapter 6, verse 25, says, "Take no thought for your life, what ye shall eat, or what ye shall drink; nor yet for your body what ye shall put on."

In his book, *My Utmost for His Highest*, Oswald Chambers says, "Take no thought . . . don't take the pressure of forethought upon yourself." He goes on to say, "Worrying means that we do not think that God can look after the practical details of our lives." Those are pretty strong words for our culture since we have to have pills for everything often due to too much worry and anxiety.

In the *Crossword Puzzle Dictionary* by Merriam-Webster, the following are some of the other words given for worry: *fret, fuss, gnaw, goad, pain, stew, annoy, afflict, anguish, disturb, oppress, torment, trouble*, and so many more. Do any of these fit us? If you are like most of the human race, everyone has some degree of this malady. So often in life, it's not the big things that happen to us that kill our happiness, but the ongoing stew that we give to all the little details that nag us and keep us from having the best life we could enjoy.

CHAPTER 10

If I Make a Mistake, I Correct It and Move On

I N THE BOOK I've mentioned earlier, *Failing Forward*, it talks about the way you view failure. It encourages you to look at the positive aspects of failure as a learning experience. In the game of life as in any game, it is always a game of ups and downs. I have yet to find a team that is always winning. At some point they fail, learn from it, and move on after having learned to correct their mistakes.

Mike Brescia from *www.thinkrightnow.com* says, "When someone messes up, the critics are ready with the jeers. But when they make the exact same mistake, they hide it, not wanting anyone to know." So when you let someone down, or when you're feeling bad about yourself, or when you're enjoying too much success or happiness, what do many people do? Knock you down a peg or two. Criticize you. Make up ugly lies about you.

No encouragement, no feeling good for your success, no pat on your back for a job well done, nope. Just hit you where it hurts. That is why most people think so badly of themselves. Because we take all the "no you can't's" we've heard in life, the "You're not good enough" and we internalize them and believe them.

This may not be what you experienced; however, many people don't ever recover from criticism or a failure that paralyzes them rather than moving them forward.

Over thirty years ago, my family moved from Oklahoma to New Orleans and adopted the New Orleans's Saints football team. Each year as so many New Orleans fans did, we always felt that this could be the year of opportunity for the Saints to go to the Super Bowl. Each year, they failed.

Yet, we never gave up the idea that one day they would do it—go to the Super Bowl. In 2007, they went into the final four play-offs for the first time and reignited the excitement for our team—the Saints.

Although many years had passed in getting to this point, the Saints organization kept learning from their mistakes moving forward and voila—the Saints were a great success. Even though everyone was disappointed that we didn't go to the Super Bowl, we had accomplished so much more than anyone would have ever dreamed with a new coach and many new players.

The Saints went on to win the Superbowl in 2010. There was a victory parade with over a million people who stood in frigid winter temperature accompanied by a strong cold wind. We all were so elated with the Saints' win that the strong wind and cold could not put a damper on our victory parade.

So it is with our lives. Each day brings new opportunities to learn from our failures that make such good teachers. In conversation with my son after his daughters had lost to me in ping-pong, I said that failure is sometimes a better teacher than success because it causes us to evaluate our mistakes. He replied aptly, "Yes, but there need to be successes also so that they don't get discouraged." I then remembered that in any sport his twin daughters had played, they were very successful—even in ping-pong.

I was lucky to have beaten them in ping-pong. When they moved to Amarillo, they were invited to be on a special team for basketball because of their abilities. And yet, it was good that they didn't always win. It would be the spark to move them forward to learn more.

As has been said, "It's not how many times you are knocked down, but whether you get back up and go again." After Katrina hit, it stunted our New Orleans economy at first. After the catastrophic storm, a CEO of one of our companies was unable to move forward and only saw doom. Another CEO asked him, "Where are you looking?" He encouraged him to move forward and quit looking at the tragedy—to do what was necessary to make his company work through the challenge. Today, many months after the catastrophe, his company has thrived. He and his company could have let the water submerge his future.

CHAPTER 11

I'll Like You If You Want

I N THE TV program *American Idol*, the candidates who show that they care about the audience stand out. There is instant connection between the singer and the audience. You can see it in the live audience's response to the singer's enthusiasm. Some fake it pretty well, but eventually their real feelings about the audience come through.

"I'll Like You if You Want" is my way of saying, "If you want to have people respond positively to you, you must first respond positively to people." It certainly must be a genuine expression of you—I like you and would enjoy becoming a friend. In Dale Carnegie's book *How to Win Friends and Influence People* his theme of reaching out in friendship echoes—I'll like you if you want.

There are some people who do not like people and won't respond, but there are very few people who are like this. The phrase "If you want a friend, you must first be a friend" underscores the idea, "Cast your bread upon the waters, and it will come back to you." Remember, this is the long-term look at being amicable and looking to be a friend of anyone who wants to reciprocate.

In the first grade, my son walked to school with his buddies but came home complaining that his friends ran ahead of him on the way to school. My wife wisely said, "If you want to be with them, you must run also." It solved his problem as he learned to keep pace with his friends. It is true as well in having friends.

A book or quotations said, "If you have one or two true friends in a lifetime you are very fortunate." A true friend sticks closer than a brother comes from the wisdom of the ages. You know who your real friends are when you have a calamity in your life. Then your true and caring friends arise.

Likewise, you know who you really care about when one of your friends experiences a calamity. Your response measures your true friendship with the person. Of course there are some impossible circumstances that must be taken into consideration in measuring friends and your friendship.

So then, if you want friends, you must reach out in friendship. Whoever does not reach back for friendship, that's OK, but there will be those that will reach back.

Here is an exercise that would be worth doing.

Name ten friends that you have known over the last ten years.

_____

_____

_____

_____

_____

_____

_____

How many have you kept in touch with?

Of those you have kept in touch with, who could you count on to come immediately to your aid in a calamity?

_____

Of those you feel would help you through a severe problem, how often do you touch base with them?

Then, have you expressed to them what they mean to you?

After I wrote these questions, I was shocked at how I answered the questions. It helped me realize how little time I spend in cultivating ongoing friendships. Stay tuned with me since I decided after writing this chapter that I need to change my ways in nurturing friendships. I have just been too busy doing other things. Anyone can pick up the phone and make one phone call a day to stay in touch with those you love and love you.

As I started to finish this chapter, I was motivated to call my cousin regarding her ill sister. I left a voice mail. It is a start to be true to what I am writing. You too can stop for a minute and make some attempt to communicate with someone who needs to hear from you. You will have a much fulfilled day if you do.

Although I diverted somewhat from the subject in this chapter, it relates to keeping the relationships that we build. All your life these relationships will become some of the most important matters in your life.

My wife builds long-lasting relationships by being the facilitator of reconnecting with her friends of long ago. She sends birthday cards, anniversary cards and calls them several times a year. Even where she has worked she keeps up with some with her work friends by scheduling a dinner from time to time. She then takes pictures and shares them with those that attended. Although it takes effort and time, she enjoys those times when they reconnect.

There certainly is someone you can reconnect with; the joy you get by communicating with your friend will far exceed the effort it takes to do.

CHAPTER 12

I'm Governed by My Thinking

IF YOU THINK you will succeed, you probably will. Conversely, if you think you will not, you probably will not. You see what goes on inside your head dictates to a large degree what dreams will eventually become true. There is certainly more to dreaming and seeing yourself successful, but this is where it starts.

The dream of man going to the moon started with the eye in the heavens wondering if man could fly to the moon. The scientists had to dream and then began researching the possibility of flight to the moon.

Going back in time, the Wright brothers in their garage bike shop believed that they could engineer a machine that would take flight. They researched the best area to launch their dream. The Atlantic winds blowing on the beaches of Kitty Hawk, North Carolina, seemed the ideal place to loft their dream. They traveled in the air only several hundred feet, but flight was forever born.

My uncle did not graduate from high school but had an inventor's mind. He saw possibilities that people around missed. During the war he worked in the shipbuilding industry on the West coast. After having experience in working with fiberglass, he invented a fiberglass fishing rod along with ways to paint the rod. Years later moving to Michigan, he started his own company building fishing rods.

When the rod business became over competitive, he began to build high-line fiberglass poles. Orders took off, and the rest is history. Over the years his business has been very successful. What's the point of this story? You must implement your dreams. Test them out and research them. Then move forward believing in yourself and your dream.

While in management at a brokerage, an agent of mine in his twenties invented a method of shoring houses. Although he was licensed to sell real estate, I encouraged him in his entrepreneurship toward his invention. He had a dream to have his own shoring company. Today, he is one of the leading shoring companies in New Orleans.

He conceived the idea for the invention while watching another company shore his dad's home. He believed he could come up with a better way to shore—and he succeeded. No matter what age a person is, they can start toward their dream to fulfill it. With age comes realistic dreams, but they are still as captivating as young dreams.

The track hurdles give runners a chance to spring over the obstacles one after another. The ability to keep their speed up and loft over the hurdles adds to the challenge of running, demanding more rigorous training. The demanding stretches of any endeavor give us an opportunity to reach out to new goals and cause us to learn how to stretch toward our potential. It is often said, "Problems in life can help develop character."

You can help yourself each day by making a list of three problems that you solved.

1.

2.

3.

How did you solve them, and why were they a problem?

Then celebrate achieving a solution. Each day keep a log for at least a week.

Once you do this for a week, the chances are great you will keep up this positive reinforcement.

This will escalate in helping you solve problems.

You will grow toward reaching those important goals that you want to achieve.

CHAPTER 13

I'm Forgiven and You Are Too

FORGIVE AND BE forgiven. Very simply put in the New Testament. This is one of the most important truths to live by in the day-to-day existence. It's not the thought, "Oh, it's OK that you hurt me or did something to destroy me. I forgive you." It is the difficult decision to live every day in forgiveness of those things you did to hurt others or didn't do to help a friend or an acquaintance. Along with forgiving yourself, you must live to be ready to forgive others for their shortcomings.

There are many stories of family members who reached out to a killer who had destroyed their loved one. You say, "How could someone ever come to forgive like this." You see, it comes down to understanding how the master forgiver, Jesus Christ, reached out to those who were crucifying him, "Forgive them, for they know not what they do." Even in his dying moments he was demonstrating the ultimate in forgiveness.

Years ago, a young Christian named Dave Wilkinson exited off an interstate into a neighborhood that was known for gang murders and violence. He was living in forgiveness and felt a purpose in his life to help those who had no purpose but to kill or be killed.

He was cornered by a group of thugs who said they were going to kill him. He replied, "You do and every part of my body will tell you, I love you." They were so overcome with this that they wanted to know him and what made him different. In the following days and weeks, they came to know about the forgiveness that he was telling them about.

Living in forgiveness changes everything in a person's life. No matter what a person does to you, you have an understanding of what potential each person has, and you encourage that potential with forgiveness. It doesn't mean you overlook the hurts inflicted on you, but you deal with them in a different way. Forgiveness looks to the future and celebrates the moment.

Unforgiveness is a sort of regression. It is refusing to let go of the hurts, heartbreaks, and insults from persons. It drags the past into the moment and the future. It stifles creativity and the ability to celebrate the moment. It brings man back to the mentality of hunt or be hunted. It fogs the emotions and eliminates the power of reaching out in love. It is the twin of hate. Also there are so many side effects of unforgiveness.

Like a volcano that boils until it explodes destroying everything in its path, unforgiveness spews out it venom sooner or later. It is not a matter of, "Will it happen?" It is a matter of when.

On the other hand, the residual benefits of true forgiveness move you forward with a whole new set of values. You reach out in understanding to more people, and they often reach back. You look more toward the good in people instead of sifting through the negative of others. It is like drinking cool springwater instead of murky water.

It is a way to wake up each day with a spring in your step with the attitude you will be ready to have an attitude of forgiveness. This positive energy flow can transform your life into a life of contribution.

By now you may think this is all hype—all of the positives could not possibility come to pass. Rest assured that there will be reversals, but this inoculation of forgiveness will come back flowing through you and melting away the woes that you may be facing.

Where does the flow of forgiveness come from? It is the total surrender of your life to the principle that Jesus Christ demonstrated on the cross when he said, "Father, forgive them, for they know not what they do." He was talking about the community around him that sought to destroy him. Jesus saw beyond the physical to the spiritual and saw their spiritual need of forgiveness over their overt act of crucifying him.

This is an ongoing flow of forgiveness since our pride is desperate to drive forgiveness away and destroy the spirit of the forgiver. It is like riding a bicycle. If you stop pedaling, the bike will turn over. If you stop forgiving, your pride will cause you to fall. Spiritual health takes maintenance just like natural health takes maintenance. What is your best story of forgiveness?

Why not stop right now and write in a journal the history of the steps of forgiveness that you went through?

_____

_____

_____

_____

_____

_____

_____

_____

_____

_____

_____

Then you can recall what you did when the next opportunity comes to forgive someone who harms you in one way or another. Remember, it is not only impossible to truly forgive unless you have forgiveness flowing through you already, it will never happen without this forgiving spirit within you.

CHAPTER 14

This Is the Best Day of My Life

OFTEN WE HAVE read the story of someone who went through a near-death experience say, "Every day now is very special since I don't know if it may be my last."

In his book *Ship of Gold in the Deep Blue Sea*, Gary Kinder records words from a survivor of a shipwreck with six hundred-plus passengers.

This husband and wife were picked up out of the Atlantic, neither knowing if the other had survived. "We wept together as well as rejoiced and for several nights after we could neither of us sleep, so vivid were the scenes before us that we had passed through. My watch, my beautiful ring, wedding presents and many other things I valued from their associations were all lost. Though I shall never behold them again I still have the privilege of preserving them in memory and I have my darling husband, the most precious jewel of all." The Central America steamship went down during a vicious hurricane off the coast of North Carolina.

I once heard someone say when asked how he knew he was having a good day, "Every day when I wake up and can put my feet on the floor, I'm having a good day." He certainly learned the value of each day as a gift from God.

A friend, who I had not heard from for many years, called and left a message on my voice mail to call him. As we talked he was praising the Lord for the opportunity he now had to share the Love of Christ while he was on the dialysis machine. At the time of the conversation I had a slight headache and was trying to get rid of it. I sat down and realized that he would be praising the Lord for giving him a chance to relate to others who had migraine headaches. He would see his affliction as a means to relate to more people and share the love of Christ.

He indicated that my family and I had been on his mind, and he felt he had to call me. My spirits were lifted, and I renewed my zeal to begin each day in gratitude for life.

A song I learned while at a youth Christian camp said, "Every day is a better day when we give it to the Lord." So often I forget to honor the Lord with the gift of life and start the day off overburdened with all the things I must accomplish for the day. I forget and bring yesterday's problems and tomorrow's concerns with me as I approach the day. It is like I am clouding up a sunshiny day.

What if we added sun to a cloudy day as well as recognizing a sunny day? Wouldn't each day bring more joy to us as we traveled through each day realizing, "This is the day the Lord hath made, let us rejoice and be glad in it."

Yes, we have jobs that require focus, persistence, and discipline to accomplish what is expected of us, but the creativity to problem solving with an attitude of gratitude for the day would maximize our every effort.

The future is the distant mountains, and the past is the distant mountains where you have come from. Where you are standing is sure footing and where life is. Otherwise, it is always, a mirage, a life out there rather than a life where you are at the moment. The gift of the moment is a sure thing for you since you don't know what is around the corner of your life's experience.

A great older Christian woman Corrie ten Boom, who had been through the horrific German camps where laughter turned to smoke and little children rose to the sky in smoke, shared a theme of her life by getting beyond the terrible experience and saying, "The best is yet to be."

Another way of putting this is to say, "The best is now because it's all we have."

When a tragic unexpected event takes the lives of many people, have you heard the expression, "hug your loved ones?"

Tell your friends you love them, call your relatives and see how they are. Just share your love.

We all remember too well the tragic 9/11. Afterward, New York became a city where so many were like family. Although it didn't last for long, there were months when visitors and the community were melded together by a common American city tragedy. I'm sure that everyone left that morning thinking they would see their family or friends in the evening. The night before was the last for so many. If we could take away a principle of life here, it should remind us all to remember the time we have right now is the best time of our lives. So celebrate your day and let nothing disturb the gift of life that you have today.

Recently, I started my morning earlier than usual with a renewed zeal to let nothing disturb my spirit. I bought gas and charged for a car wash. Having just purchased coffee, the car wash was a perfect place to have time to take some relaxed sips of coffee.

As I slowly passed through the dryer, I reached for the coffee, and my car went over a drop and you guessed it, coffee went over my tie, my white shirt, and on my slacks. I stopped and made a decision. Today this coffee spill will not even be a beep on my radar screen since I had made a commitment to let nothing disturb the gift of life for that day.

In listening to a tape by Dr. Wayne Dyer, he gave a moving story of a spiritual leader who was verbally attacked for several days. The person who had been brutal to him asked, "I have been brutal to you verbally, but you have not let it bother you. How can you do that?" You see, today sets the stage for the next day. If you want to live life today as the best day of your life, you must remember that you do not have to accept any gift that is bad, and you do not have to own those gifts that are negative.

On a day that a storm brought flooding to the streets of New Orleans and Metairie, my brother parked his Toyota in front of our Metairie house for safety, while he and his wife traveled on Amtrak. Our street flooded. My neighbor saw the Toyota parked and called saying that she thought the water had gone into my brother's vehicle. I had insisted that he not leave the key for me since we would be gone when he got back.

We had the salesman from Pascagoula (where the car was purchased) telephone the manager of the parts department in Metairie and convince him to cut a key that would only open the car door. It was almost closing time for everyone so I rushed over to the Toyota dealer as they were closing the parts department for the weekend.

As I opened the door of my brother's Toyota, my mind was racing with what I would find. I quickly reached for the floorboard carpet to inspect. It was dry. I had been calling my brother to keep him posted on my progress. He was elated and so grateful for all that I had done to take care of this problem. I was thanking the Lord that it was dry. If the water had risen another inch, it would have gone into the car.

This day seemed to be going bad but turned out to be a great ending. Even if water had reached the inside of the car, I knew that I would take care of it. Getting a key made from a Toyota dealer on Friday with only minutes from closing was a gift. I told my wife I would kiss this key since it opened the door to a solution.

Isn't this just like most all of our days? So if we have the attitude that this is the best day of my life, we are inviting a success attitude no matter what happens to us good or bad. It helps us creatively deal with situations that otherwise might trip us up.

I'm reminded of the disciples and Jesus out in the Sea of Galilee. When the storm roared in leaving the disciples wrestling for their lives, Jesus was asleep as the boat rocked up and down. Awakened by the disciples, he calmed the seas. All was well with the disciples as they looked out over the calm ripple of the sea. How many times have we wrestled with problems letting them dictate to us what kind of a day we would have?

No matter what is going on outside of us, we can choose to be calm in the midst of the storm because we have the gift of another day. While I was growing up, our family would usually take a trip from Starkville, Mississippi, to visit relatives in Kansas. They lived on farms, which my two brothers and I enjoyed like Disney World. It was our farm experience to explore the wide open spaces on horses, pickup trucks, and tractors used for plowing. While on the fourteen-hour trip, our anticipation grew as we neared the first farmhouse out of Wellington, Kansas. My dad would pretend to take Mom's pulse as we neared her sister's house.

Our time was spent with enjoying one another, eating together, and going over the farm having the best time of our lives. Each visit was memorable. What if we were to build up anticipation for each day wondering what new things the Lord will bring into our lives?

Earlier I mentioned that the story of traveling up Pike's Peak mountain and learned that the unfolding beauty of the travel was the main thing. The anticipation of arriving at the top kept us going, but I found out that the journey was the real deal. Again, it's good to be reminded that this moment and this day is the best day of my life. This is the real deal. The tomorrow that we anticipate may never come, and the yesterdays are already gone—so today is the gift that we have now. So this is the best day of my life!

Make a list of the best days of your life.

_____
_____
_____
_____
_____

Go back into your childhood, adolescence, or adulthood and remember the simple things that could be listed as the best days of your life.

_____
_____
_____
_____
_____

List those things that you are putting off but would love to do.

_____
_____
_____
_____
_____

Start today with the easiest to do.

Go to the next thing that you could do during the week ahead.

Make a habit of assessing those things you would like to do. Realize that they all will not come to your mind in an instant.

Keep a record of those that you have done on your list.

Go further and journal these things that you do that are on your list.

Share this with one of your close friends and encourage them to do also.

CHAPTER 15

I'm on a Mission to Share that You Are Like Me and We Are Enough

E VERYONE LIVES WITH a set of values. They may be much different from other people's values, but you own them. We are alike in that all of us have beliefs that drive us. We may not even be aware what they are and where we derived them, but they come out in our daily living.

Also, our lives are alike as described in Maslow's hierarchy of unmet needs. All of us are somewhere on the staircase of unmet needs. The first unmet need Maslow gives is the survival mode. Until we have enough to eat, a place to sleep, all the other needs we have are put on hold. The next one Maslow lists is security. When we reach the first unmet need this is the one that kicks in.

We want to know that we can remain secure and that all will be well. This need is followed by social needs. We want to have friends and fit in. This unmet need sees us joining an organization of some sort. Once we feel secure that we fit with family or someone or group, the next step that Maslow lists is the ego.

Here we want others to know that we have achieved. We desire recognition and acknowledgment. We want to know that we are appreciated for our contribution.

The last unmet need is self-actualization. We want to actualize our personality and be who we are. We are not worried about what other people think but what we think we want to do and accomplish.

We can move up and down the staircase of unmet needs according to what's happening to us. If we get a terminal illness then we go back to survival—just staying alive becomes the most important need.

From Maslow's hierarchy of needs, we learn that we are like each other. We might be on different steps of the hierarchy, but we are all on the same staircase. We will all go up and down the staircase according to the unmet needs at times in life. Any one of these steps is OK. As we accept where we are on the staircase, we can accept others as to where they may be also.

The first chapter dealt with "I'm enough." We are in a culture that places so much on looks and fashion that tremendous stress is placed on performance. Somehow we may overlook how much we are alike and always look for our differences.

In my study of theology, I learned that God has placed a vacuum in everyone. We are forever trying to fill that vacuum. Until God fills it for us, we are all struggling to fill it.

So from this truth, we see that we are all on a journey seeking to fill the vacuum.

My mission then is to tell you that this truth is the foundation of a peaceful life. This truth is brought out in the constitution that says that we are all created equal and are endowed by our creator. This truth echoes the truth that your acceptance of who you are and that you are enough are two of the most valuable truths you will ever grasp.

CHAPTER 16

Take a Look Outside You

S O OFTEN WE are an island without any company. We tend to look through the lens of "What's in it for me.?" In fact, in customer service principles, this is the way we service our customers well by understanding what they are most interested in "What's in it for me?" So with this in mind, it is natural for us to remain with this as our method of operating. As we mature, we begin to observe that the world doesn't revolve around us—that others are important.

Looking outside ourselves to the needs and interests of others becomes important in the maturing process of adulthood. This can become stifled if during the formative years a person has all "wants" realized. Such persons can get the idea that they are the center of the universe and that what they want, not what they need, is the most important thing in life.

You have seen children that have been given so much during their early years that gifts become expected and rarely appreciated. Things become a surrogate form of love. These children grow to center their lives on getting things and never getting enough. No matter what they have, it is never enough, as well as the expectation that they should have more.

Having wealth or the lack thereof makes no difference when the attitude of looking outside you to the needs and cares of others becomes important. There is a peace and satisfaction that prevails everything about a person with a giving attitude.

When in college, I went to Detroit on a student mission trip. While there, I met a group of church people who extended their love and shared meals with our team of student missionaries. In their homes we were treated like royalty although the families were very poor. Oddly enough, I only remembered how rich they were in giving their time, food, and love to us while we were visiting. If I had many lifetimes, I would never forget their altruistic attitudes toward life.

Often after opening the presents at Christmas time, I noticed that although the living room was full of presents for our grandchildren, they were playing with the boxes. Their values were different from ours. At each Christmas for years, I realized that after the mad rush to open presents, they wanted our attention and time spent with them. The greatest gift was the love and care that we gave each of the grandchildren.

Recently, I got a call from someone I had known in a church over fifteen years ago. He called and chatted as if it were only yesterday and thanked me for the contribution I had made in his life. I had taught him and the church a chorus "It's Amazing What Praising Can Do." He called another day shortly after the first call and started with this song. I couldn't believe he was giving back his joy of our friendship. His call and song will remain a gift for a lifetime.

I wonder how many persons that we come in contact with are looking for a way out of their prisons of self-indulgence. Maybe we could offer a word of encouragement and direct them on a path of new freedom.

Looking outside of ourselves to helping others and being concerned for their welfare might also free us from our own selves. I remember one of the happiest times of my life was when I was helping someone move their belongings since they couldn't help themselves.

Take a look at the number of people from all over the country and world who have volunteered to come and help people rebuild their homes and lives after Katrina. Almost daily I heard of heroic efforts of people who lived far away from New Orleans came and gave their time and how this blessed their lives.

While my wife and I were displaced to the DC area due to Katrina, we joined a church. We were introduced to a group of people who had just been down to New Orleans feeding the displaced families. They stayed at two-week intervals, took a break to return home to Virginia, and then they went back to New Orleans to help. They were invigorated in spirit by being able to give away their time and talent to feed thousands of displaced Katrina victims.

My brother and his wife joined a group from North Carolina that came to the Gulf coast and helped a church and their families get back on their feet. They cleaned, rebuilt, and helped with the spiritual rebuilding of the pastors' congregation. But they went further than the congregation.

When they learned of anyone in the community that needed help, they began to help them. Even two years after the storm, they still came back to complete the task of helping rebuild the community.

When life is over, the lives that we touch with love and help will be the only legacy we leave that will continue to live on. All the wealth that we have gained is of no use to us anymore. A life full of giving then becomes the richest life. The New Testament states it so well. Store up riches in heaven so it will always be there. Don't spend life with an attitude of getting but of giving—and certainly this is talking about giving yourself away to people as much as things.

John D. Rockefeller was told that he did not have very long to live. Being wealthy, he began giving most of his wealth to charitable organizations to make good use of his fortune. Surprisingly enough, in the process of giving, he regained his health and stated that he was glad that he had given most of his wealth away. Do you think that his benevolent attitude in the midst of dying might have helped change his medical condition? I think so! It is in giving that we find the real meaning of life.

Part of the verse of a poem says, "It is in giving that we are born to eternal life." In a sense, the contributions that John D. Rockefeller made will live on for centuries.

Beethoven, one of the great composers, wrote the ninth symphony when he was in his eighties. It is called the "Ode to Joy." He was nearly blind and had lost most of his hearing, but the joy he brought to us will live on forever. The symphony speaks about the joy of sharing with each other as brothers and sisters. Thankfully, Beethoven shared this composition to us for all time. It will forever be a gift to anyone who hears it. It is a call to give the gift of you away.

Another great composer, Handel, composed the "Hallelujah Chorus" found in the *Messiah* composition. As a tradition founded by the King of

England who stood when he first heard the chorus, everyone now stands when the chorus begins. What a gift Handel gave us with this chorus that lifts us out of our mundane existence and transports us to new heights.

The *Sound of Music* musical story grew out of World War II. It is a testament that out of tragedy and the worst of times, you still can give something that can be a gift. Sometimes a smile can change the countenance of a person who is feeling isolated. A word of encouragement can do wonders when people feel no one cares. A deed of kindness that is out of the natural overflow of a person's life can turn a distraught person around and give them hope.

CHAPTER 17

Your Hope of the Future

I TALKED WITH a friend of mine whose nineteen-year-old grandchild wanted to get a book, *The Five People You Meet in Heaven*. She then wanted my friend to read the book so they could discuss it together. I marveled that this nineteen-year-old teenager was so interested in the afterlife. This story challenged my interest to look onto the hills where help comes from—God. This is hope.

How do you define hope? Some of the sayings regarding hope are: Hope things work out for you; I hope I will get the new job, I hope that . . . and you fill in the blank. We use hope as a good luck charm in our conversation so many times. However, hope is more certain than good luck or good fortune.

It is based upon promises that are from truth. A great hymn, the "Solid Rock," has been a favorite of mine to internally sing in the morning, during the day, and at night before I go to sleep. An excerpt from the hymn is, "My hope is built on nothing less than Jesus blood and righteousness." The chorus says, "On Christ the solid rock I stand, all other else is sinking sand."

This hymn expresses an action toward standing on solid ground as opposed to taking a chance that things will work out. It positions a person with a real hope that will stand up to the worst of circumstances and gives one something to look forward to. It is hope that creates solid footing on every part of our lives giving us freedom to live fully every day without the anxiety that so often fills our days. Of course in our human situation, we may revert to the habit of worry causing anxiety, however, when we refocus our attention to the hills from where our help comes from, the worries melt away.

I met a veteran from the Korean War who stated, when he got up out of the foxhole to charge the enemy, he would say, "Lord, I may see you in a minute." His hope was not hoping he would survive since he already knew that his hope was trusting in the Lord. What a testimony this has been to remind me, that whatever comes my way, my hope is not on the outcome of my situation, but on the sure footing of hope that I have.

Living in post-Katrina days, the news, talk shows, magazines were all on the same chorus—things were not going well in the recovery. Everywhere you turned, you were bombarded with the hopelessness of the situation. In the midst of this, one Sunday at church there was a group from a church in California. They had been sending help continuously. It reminded me that as the saying goes, "inch by inch is a chinch" not yard by yard.

While driving through one of the hardest hit areas, I saw a group of athletes who were giving their spring break to the recovery effort in Chalmette, another hard-hit area. They were all wearing the same colored T-shirts as a symbol of their unified cause—helping New Orleans get back on her feet. These young people will never be the same as they have given of themselves to people who have gone through a disaster.

While looking around on the Internet, I discovered a therapy called "hope therapy." I recalled the classic book, *Man's Search for Meaning*. The book describes what happened in some of the death prisons during World War II. The author, Viktor Frankl, a psychiatrist, was a prisoner in one of these camps. He observed that some prisoners of war died, but it appeared physically they should have lived. Others lived who looked physically like there was no way they could survive.

He wrote about this and came up with a therapy called "logo therapy." It is in my opinion; this logo therapy is a sister to hope therapy. His thesis was when persons lose meaning in their lives, they find no reason to live. When those without meaning were in the prisons for so long, they gave up hope.

We have all heard stories about people who outlived the time doctors gave them since they wanted to stay alive for some special event—like a son or daughter's graduation.

CHAPTER 18

Communication Is the Key to Good Relationships

A T THE SCENE of an accident that I witnessed, the faulty driver said she didn't see a red light. The victim driver, who was quite shaken, looked to me to validate her side. When the light turned green, she was driving through the intersection when this vehicle broadsided her and jolted both her and her passenger.

In talking with the guilty driver, I assured her the sun was probably making it difficult to see the red light. She looked terrified and realized then that she must have been mistaken and focused on the two ladies who were in the other car.

We all sometimes see reality as we want and don't stop to find the truth about something. The reason that there are so many lawyers and courts is that the parties in court have different views about what happened.

At the homeowners' association board meeting, one of the members raved on and on about concerns that weighed heavy on her. Being in charge, I asked that we deal with one at a time and the weightiest concerns first.

In her mind everything was in disarray. My prior experiences taught me that she lived on a steady diet of extreme exaggerations.

The board narrowed down her concerns and made a simple plan of action on each of her concerns. Although she wanted to continue, we agreed we had tackled the most urgent things she had presented.

Had we not clearly communicated to her to focus on each concern with a plan of action, we could have stayed all night hearing her complaints without any resolutions to the problems she presented. You see, not only did we serve her in listening, but we responded properly dealing with each concern.

Most of the problems with corporations, families, nations, and other organizations are due to incomplete communication. We live in a culture saturated with communication through e-mail, text messaging, and cell phones. The downside is that so many communications do not convey what we intended to communicate. By the time a reply comes to you, the gap of communication can widen. Then there is the time lapse between the sent messages.

Negative feelings can have entered into the message, and as the message is read over and over, it is misunderstood over and over. It can take days and even weeks to resolve a misunderstood e-mail or a voice mail.

Although it is easier to have this happen using e-mail, the phone can be a big stumbling block to true communication.

Someone can call and have an unhappy message on your voice mail. You then can fire a reply back only to get a voice mail. By the time the two of you talk, there is an emotional smoke screen that you have to talk through.

So why has our culture made it so difficult to understand each other with all these fast ways of communication? A staff member called me the other day asking if I had the projector that I had used the day before. I replied, "No, I delivered it back to the tech department since it was to be used by someone the next day." Rather than e-mail or voice mail looking for it, I went through our company asking if anyone knew where the projector might be.

I found it. Someone else had gone and picked it up from the tech department without letting the tech director know. I then found the person who needed it and explained who had it and why. She thought that I still had it and just didn't put it back in the tech department. My walking around and doing face-to-face communication solved a big problem without having to spend hours going through the e-mail or voice mail process.

Deborah Tannen, PhD, tells in her book *You Just Don't Understand* about a couple who had a communication problem over a very simple encounter while traveling in their car. "The woman had asked, 'Would you like to stop for a drink?' Her husband had answered, truthfully, 'No,' and they hadn't stopped.'"

He was later frustrated to learn that his wife was annoyed because she had wanted to stop for a drink. He wondered, 'Why didn't she just say what she wanted? Why did she play games with me?' The wife, I explained, was annoyed not because she had not gotten her way, but because her preference had not been considered. From her point of view, she had shown concern for her husband's wishes, but he had shown no concern for hers."

How would you replay the previous conversation if you were in this situation? I read this last paragraph to my wife, and she reminded me that when I ask if it's hot in here, I'm really saying, "Dear, would you adjust the thermostat?"

What we think we said many times is not what the other person heard. For example, in conversation at a committee meeting, a member stated that I did not want to give a worker a raise. Earlier I had brought up the fact that one of our workers had been with us for many years but had not received any significant raise. I said, "No, that's not true. The budget keeper said that we would have to wait until next year where we could put it in the budget." Everyone in the group sat silent so I didn't pursue it. However, at this next meeting it appeared that since I didn't press for the increase until next year I was not for the increase. I had to clarify my position that had been taken the wrong way. It was quickly resolved by the group afterward.

We all tend to filter hearing from our point of view. It is when we truly try to understand what the intent is that communication can begin. Our prejudices scream out over what's being said and often cause us to interpret what was said through our own eyes.

This subject has volumes written on it. So this chapter is to whet your appetite on the communication subject. One of the studies I learned about is that only around 30 percent of communication is verbal. It states that about 70 percent of communication is body language. This suggests to me that if you want to increase your chances of good communication, you may want to try to do it face-to-face.

This accents the loss of good communication so often when it is by e-mail, voice mail, text messaging, and phone. Although the phone is much better than the other methods mentioned, the best is face-to-face when you can pay attention to what the other person is saying and observe body language. There may be times when body language does not match what is being said. Communication is achieved 70 percent thorough body language, 20 percent in how you say it, and 10 percent on what you say. There is no way you can completely communicate 100 percent what you intended to say through e-mail, text messaging, or even the phone.

There are times when electronic communication is appropriate and face-to-face communication is impossible; however, if understanding is critical, it would save time to meet face-to-face or through video conferencing in order to have good communication. You want to come away completely understanding what each intended to communicate.

Consequently, I began bringing together truths to help persons build a solid foundation to deal positively with challenges as they come. I was amazed how much it helped me in my day-to-day activities.

My hope is that you will benefit from each chapter and apply some of the principles to your life. Start out and read the whole book. Then go back and key in on those truths that you feel are applicable to you. Share with your close friends what you are learning, which will reinforce what you have learned.

Remember that the beliefs you carry now are the accumulation of a lifetime and that to replace some beliefs that are holding you back from moving forward in your life may take much time. So be patient with yourself and also be patient with those around you.

You will notice that life can be a new joy to you, and each day can begin with new enthusiasm.

A book I read many years ago, *Enthusiasm Makes the Difference*, is true. However, you must build a new foundation for your life to support enthusiasm. Again, I hope that you can get up each day looking forward to see what the day may bring, knowing that good or bad; you are adequate to face the challenge.

And challenges are given to us where we can grow. If you are to maintain strength and muscle tone in your body, you must have a time several times a week where you work out. It can be walking, swimming, playing golf, any type of workout to challenge your physical. We all know to do it, yet I challenge you to start today doing something physical to challenge yourself, even if it is ten minutes. Then move on to add minutes to each workout.

Also, as you work out, increase challenge to the body—as in swimming, during the swim add speed to the ten to twenty minutes that you swim. The result is a feeling of energy and accomplishment. This translates to other endeavors you take on. You feel you can do—you receive a spirit of confidence as you challenge your body, now you can successfully challenge the mind.

I now try to be proactive in helping around the house with work that my wife would normally do. I look for household chores to help out with before I'm asked.

I realize that I take ownership in the house looking clean. Also, with renewed energy, I take the garbage out and use it to do arm lifts as I walk to the dumpster. My biceps like my garbage trip.

This helps me feel that the time is put to good use rather than feeling that time is being lost when taking out the garbage.

Also, I lump together tasks like sweeping, vacuuming, and mopping and try to work up a sweat while doing all three. This is a great way to challenge the body and reduce a few ounces.

DARREL HOOVER

CHAPTER 19

When You're Down, Look Up

THERE WAS A gentleman who was incarcerated for taking a life—a convicted murderer. After spending many years in isolation, he heard someone tell him, "Look up." He took this as a sign from the Lord to turn his life over to the Lord. After he served his time, he joined a faith church and sat on the first row. While attending the same church, I noticed that he was celebrating more than anyone else. After getting to know him, I realized that every moment was precious to him, especially since he was walking in faith. One day he gave me a gift of a shirt that he had hand sewn. He had learned the skill while in prison.

The shirt had wavy stitches in the front down the middle. In just a few weeks he passed away. I learned that he had died of cancer. That shirt had been painfully made for me. It took on a new meaning to realize that while he had time, he was sewing a shirt as a gift to me. His faith had moved mountains for him even though he had little time left here on earth. His memory will forever be etched on my mind. The short time he spent outside the prison was spent in celebration of his remaining life as he lived with the type of faith that could move mountains.

I visited the hospital to see one of our company's contractors who had been in a severe motorcycle accident. One of his leg bones was shattered leaving him without much of a leg muscle. He had been confined to one position—on his back for one month, when I visited with him.

I asked him if he would ride again, since this was his passion. He laughed and said, "I can't wait to get back on the motorcycle." He had crashed his motorcycle because there was no signage on a split in the road at a construction site. Therefore, he felt the accident was a fluke. He was not about to let a near-death experience kill his dream.

I reflect back to the times that a good word of encouragement to someone helped them keep working on their dream. I also remember persons who said, "If someone had encouraged me toward my dreams, I would have gone another direction to fulfill my dreams."

A hero of mine works for our company. He was in his prime as a manager of one of our branches when he was diagnosed with multiple sclerosis. It paralyzed most of his body from the neck down. His attitude is to make the best of a bad situation. He became a webmaster, a graphics artist, and a great support for our company. Rather than requiring someone to drive him around, he had special electronics put in his van so he could maintain a normal life.

His sweetheart has stayed with him all these years going to every function with him. She has a radiant personality and enjoys life. She is also a hero. She has been his encouragement. Her support has helped him be an overcomer.

When you are faced with some devastating news that will impact your life whether it is a health issue, job loss, or loss of your possessions, you just remember not to focus on your loss but look at each day as a gift and start moving toward the future.

As I remember, Albert Einstein's father and son witnessed a traumatic event in their lives. As they stood there watching their barn—their living—burn to the ground, he told Albert to get his mother since she had never seen such a fire. Then without stopping with the conversation said, "Well let's get to work and start rebuilding this barn." Wow, what an attitude! He was looking toward the future knowing that they could recover as long as they didn't focus on their past loss.

CHAPTER 20

Share with Your Best Friend

HOPEFULLY, YOUR PARTNER is your best friend. Recently, a minister challenged the audience to read the Bible, pray, and worship for an hour for seven days. My wife and I took the challenge.

We worshipped about an hour every day for seven days. The spiritual benefits were terrific, however, the time each day started us communicating with each other in a more meaningful way. Instead of the couch potato time watching television, we began to help each other by listening to what was going on with the other.

The times were so meaningful during those seven days, that afterward we kept having our worship, Bible reading, and prayer time. Although we are not rigid about the amount of time spent, we try to always have time to spend in Bible reading, worship, and prayer.

No matter what you have done during the day, a time with your friend, partner, or anyone else can be some of the most valuable time in your life. TV programs can take a lot of your time, but meaningful times spent in sharing can help celebrate the gift of friendship.

Also, these times can recharge your emotional battery. When your battery in your car is used up and doesn't have a source to replenish its electrical energy, it goes dead. Your car stops. So it is with your life; you need a source of energy replacement, both spiritual and emotional. You can regain part of this energy through meaningful sharing.

Every day is a new start, a new year, a new beginning. So how do you start to have a turnaround in your life?

1. Go back re-reading for six weeks the chapters that directly relate to your situation.

2. You already have a script you are living by, which may be holding you back from experiencing a fulfilled life—a life using your talents and skills to the fullest.

3. In order for you to move forward in your life, you will need to begin to write a new script. The previous chapters were written with you in mind, helping you realize that your birth was important because there is no one like you. You bring into the world new creativity—a unique person.

4. Psalm 139 is one of the most important chapters in the Bible since it affirms the value of you and the forethought that the Lord had for you. It would be a good idea to read this once a week for at least a year to experience an understanding of how valuable you are.

5. Take an inventory of your friends. Are they affirming to you as a person or do they tear you down? Many times persons gravitate toward others who are negative because they are negative about themselves.

6. Make it a point to initiate new friendships that mutually build up. You tend to take up the attitudes, personalities, and the values of those around you.

7. If you grew up in a family that tore you down, you are a likely candidate for a counselor, a friend, a minister, or someone that you trust to share your life to gaining new insights in how to get through a negative family past.

8. Sometimes a relative who cares about you can be a great help. Initiate a relationship with them where you can trust them in a sharing relationship.

9. Deviate from your regular schedule to take care of yourself. For example, if you are in a job that requires minute-by-minute concentration, get out for lunch where you can restore your energy. During the day, take breaks away from what you are doing to relieve you of the stress that starts to weigh upon you.

10. Take time to dream, to meditate, and to let your mind rest where your creativity can kick in.

11. When you are by yourself and the negatives start to invade your mind, imagine that the thoughts are on a slide presentation. Delete this slide and go to a thought (slide) that is uplifting, good, healthy giving you refreshment. You see, your life is made up like a slide presentation, so pull up the slides that bring you joy, laughter, and are uplifting.

12. An example of the previous point, I have a memory of interacting with an ex-convict who spent most of his life in the penitentiary. You will recall reading about him in chapter 19. He was released in the twilight of his life when I got to know him. In church he was the happiest in the congregation enjoying his freedom physically as well as in the spirit. Go back and read this inspiring story.

13. Now go back in your life and start to make a list of the moments in your life that brought you joy. We all have them even though you may have to meditate many times to remember the uplifting times in your life.

14. Sometimes we get distraught enough that it's like the blinds are pulled down; we are unable to see the good times and reexperience them. You may need a jumpstart to get you going similar to a battery jump on your car. Immediately get help. Go back and review no. 7 and move forward.

15. Sometimes you have a stronghold in your life that is disabling you. Also, you may have a recurring disappointment that keeps you paralyzed from moving forward in your life. If these recurring memories keep coming to you, by all means seek someone you trust to talk with about this. It is advisable to go further by seeking counsel with a trusted professional. It may take a few visits to get rid of recurring memories; other times it might take months and years depending on the type of problem that keeps you from going forward.

16. Make a list of your dreams that you would like to do. Freely write what comes into your mind without censorship as to whether you think it could be realized. Filter the negative voices that block your creativity in thinking about what you would like to do. Many times a

near-death experience for someone wakes them up to reenergize their dreams. Don't let that happen to you, but set aside a time and place for dreaming.

17. A good way to mark progress on turning around your life is to journal. This of course is not a diary but a log each day of your thoughts, ideas, things learned, and your dreams. Out of this will come thoughts or dreams that surprise you—which you were not aware of. It is also a good reminder of where you have been as you reread the journal. Also, some have used this to help them through a crisis or through posttraumatic stress syndrome. However, the majority of us will greatly benefit from writing, just to know more about ourselves and our dreams.

18. Develop a spirit of giving, reaching out to family, friends, relatives, and those in need.

19. Now is the time for you to write your future. Start with each chapter and write freely why you are valuable. This is for your eyes only, not for bragging but for building up a good foundation of you as a valuable human being.

20. The following exercise may be the most important part of this book. I've given you some space after you reread each chapter to write your chapter whether brief or whether lengthy. Remember, this is to help you build that all-important foundation. There may be times that you compare yourself to someone who is so much more skilled in a certain area. Stop! Kick this out of your mind and build on who you are. You can learn from others in your areas of interest, but never start comparing yourself to someone who is so much better than you in certain areas. Comparing yourself to others is the most destructive thing you can do. Start now writing your chapter.

_____

_____

_____

_____

_____

_____

_____

_____

_____

_____

_____

_____

21. If you have difficulty moving ahead with positive feelings about yourself, the chapters that you write for yourself will be very important to reread. You can build yourself up to having a great day before the day is over. I have experienced this many times in my life. You can get on a downward spiral very quickly, especially when there is so little encouragement all around you.

22. Don't expect a thank you on anything you accomplish but be gracious if you do get a thank you. It is a good idea to have a file on those that do thank you for any reason. Go to that file and remember that you are important to people.

23. Reignite relationships with family, relatives, and friends. Be on the lookout for new opportunities for building friendships. List those people you would like to reconnect with.

_____

_____

_____

_____

_____

_____

24. John Maxwell's book _Thinking for a Change_ is great for learning to change your thinking toward a productive life, a life where you maximize your potentials. Today, I began negating my ideas and strengths. Then I started reading John Maxwell's book, which reenergized my zeal to do my best with those strengths that I have. I could not wait to get back to the office and go to work utilizing my skills to help others realize their strengths and abilities.

25. Since life is so conditioned on the past, it is vital that each day you move forward on improving your strengths. I suggest that you make a

list of the things you want to accomplish that will help you get better. Nurture your gifts every day to help you deal with the next day in a better way. Remember to keep a journal of the ideas, the things learned, and the rewards you feel in doing a job well.

_____

_____

_____

_____

_____

_____

_____

_____

_____

_____

POSTLOGUE

AFTER TRAGEDY, WE tend to look inward and take inventory of our lives. Whether it is a national loss as in 9/11, a local loss in your area, or a personal loss, all of us have a psyche that causes us to go through stages of grief. These series of stages take different forms and different timetables, but eventually the stages are normally realized.

Psychologists suggest we go through shock, denial, grief, anger, and then acceptance. It may take weeks, months, or years; or one may never reach acceptance depending on how the person dealt with the loss.

There have been several tragedies that have affected so many in the last few years that I thought, "How can I help people build a good foundation for dealing with life during tough times?" After all, the way you view yourself and others can greatly affect the way you deal with loss.

Consequently, I began the journey to bring together truths that could help others build a solid foundation in their lives and deal positively with the challenges as they come. I was amazed how much my journey helped me in my day-to-day activities when I read again what I had written. Hopefully, you will remember some milestones in your life that you cherish. This will assist you in your journey forward.

My hope is that you have benefited from each chapter and have applied some of the principles to your life. After you have read the whole book, go back and key in on those truths that you feel are applicable to you. Share with your close friends what you are learning to reinforce what you have learned.

Remember, the beliefs you carry now are the accumulation of your lifetime. To replace some beliefs that are keeping you from moving forward in your life may take much time. So be patient with yourself and also be patient with those around you. You will notice that life can be a new joy to you and each day can begin with new enthusiasm.

You may need a trusted friend or a counselor to give you feedback. A wise person is the one who is willing to seek help when needed, and we all at some time need help.

A book I read many years ago, *Enthusiasm Makes the Difference*, can also make a big difference in your life. However, you must build a new foundation for your life, a fresh pair of eyes to support enthusiasm. Again, I hope that you can get up each day looking forward to what the day may bring, knowing that good or bad; you are adequate to face the challenge.

In Sarah Ban Breathnach's book *A Journey to Simple Abundance* there is a chapter titled "Gratitude." Roger Evans tells the story of his wife's two bouts with cancer.

> Throughout both illnesses, she's exhibited a fundamental fearlessness. In the face of a difficult clinical prognosis, she has an admirable inner peace. She's not sad, she's not afraid of dying; she's maintained absolutely unflagging high spirits throughout this whole episode. She wakes up every day with a smile, looks at the bright side, and doesn't get caught up in depression or self-pity. You realize that everyone, sick or well, can at least try to make the choice she makes. A day is going to occur whether you fight it or not. You can choose to get caught up in the dreadful, sad negative side of it or you can treat it as a good day, a special day, the only one exactly like this you'll ever have. It's the simplest choice in the world, regardless of how you feel.

This example of looking forward to each day as a gift and knowing you are a gift motivates us to maximize our days.

Also, I encourage you to write down your own journey from this day forward. You can buy an inexpensive notebook and date it each day you make an entry. Make it a journal of your thoughts, feelings, and important events that took place each day. (This is not a diary but a way to put your heart on paper.)

I have found that you go inward to live outward. You get a sense of wholeness in a day rather than a day that may be fractured. You also can learn to better express verbally what you intended to say at times but had difficulty in expressing your thoughts out loud to someone.

And lastly, remember that change may be painful at times, but change can be the most rewarding thing you can do to better face the challenges you may have. I often remember the sentence in the Bible where Jesus says, "If I had the faith as a grain of mustard seed, I could say to this mountain, be removed" (my paraphrase). I have pondered this verse so many times so that each time I see more power in it.

Think of a tiny atom that causes a chain reaction which can cause catastrophic devastation. Then I am reminded that however small my faith is, it is powerful enough to sustain me through any challenge. If you take away only this thought from this book, it could revolutionize your life into facing challenges successfully.

Since I have been writing this book, our country has gone into a national financial crisis. I realize more than ever that the effects of losing a job, a home, and other losses can lead to the loss of who you are and the gift you bring to this planet. The master designer knows you by name and is interested in your life.

This is a time to turn to your church, your friends, your family for help—the biggest part of help can come from sharing your journey with these support groups. Instead of letting loss destroy you, seek help immediately, and move forward instead of retreating back in the doldrums of loss.

I met a young lady the other day at a library who shared about a traumatic experience she had in her life. She said that it took a lot of time to get over it, but because of the experience, she dedicated her life to helping others get through similar traumatic experiences. Perhaps your experiences could be the opportunities to help others going through similar experiences. Who knows that this could eventually help you by helping others? The writer of Romans in the New Testament helped us remember, "And we know that all things work together to them that love who love God . . . ."